101 Delicious Soups, Stews, Chowders and Broths

A cookbook of homemade recipes to suit all occasions, seasons and tastes

by Delia Fitzsimmons

Published by Triangle Circle Square Press

© Delia Fitzsimmons 2016

Table of Contents

Preface

This manual of cooking contains over a hundred different tasty soups, stews, broths and chowders. While for purposes of catchy titling, the book is entitled '101' – there are in fact a total of 117 different recipes within this book. Ample purchase is given to vegetarians and vegans, while those fond of meat will be pleased to encounter a variety of soups too. My personal emphasis is upon mutton and veal from the bone; these can however be substituted by beef or in some cases pork should your locality not have such meats available with ease. Certain versatile soups, such as tomato soup or chicken soup, receive a few variations each to appropriately tribute their versatility.

I make no pretence of this book being a fanciful manual; the recipes are simply writ upon a page ready for easy, momentary consultation. While about a quarter of the recipes find accompanying illustrations, they are not the sort to take up an entire page in designer photographic finesse. This is a simple, unpretentious manual which tells the means and order of each dish's preparation, and that is that.

The overall purpose of this recipe book is as a small pocket handbook easy to bring along should you go on holiday, visit friends, go camping, or simply need to whip up a quick soup or stew in your kitchen. I admit that the recipes are pithy and simply stated – there is no room for the fancier herbs or seasonings here, and while you may indulge in invention or elaborate upon the meals mentioned here, that is a matter for you to deliberate according to personal, private taste.

The traditional French *bouchon*, wherein soups and stews have been served for ages - Image: Trishhhh

Particular attention has been given to the French soups and stews - for it is from France that many of the best soups consumed popularly in the West originated. Despite this attention, I do not for want of description take fanciful excursions into the

French language which would only serve to baffle readers.

In addition, I've included a few unusual recipes, such as one for chocolate (Cocoa-nut) stew. These are worth trying if only to see if you happen to take fancy of the distinctive tastes. The impressive qualities of beef stew with tea as a component have gone seldom noticed in the modern day, while the process of enlivening common oatmeal with vegetables is likewise lost to the modern soup chef despite its simplicity and straightforward nutritional merits.

It is hoped that by these unique quirks, that this small recipe book has a value all its own. Although many texts have concerned certain regions – or indeed all of them – it is this cookbook's combination of the old methods and meals with the perennial favourites which I graciously hope the reader enjoys and benefits from.

Much of the instruction herein has its roots in old-fashioned principles of food preparation; there is little if any room given to artificial chemicals or flavour enhancers, and colours are expected to originate naturally. The age-old, natural flavour enhancement of cooking a soup slowly is the most favoured in aid of vivid taste, and the ingredients are all sourced from your local organic grocers and butchers.

This is essentially a book written with the uncompromising and traditional mentality of the grandmother, suspicious of the latest trends in cooking, and of modern elaborations that violate a culinary canon that dates back hundreds of years. With that in mind, let us begin by examining the archetypal nature and vital accompaniments of a truly good soup or stew entrée.

Delia Fitzsimmons – Spring 2016

Introduction to the Principles of Soups and Stews

Soups and stews, like salads, present an excellent opportunity for the cook to display good taste and judgment. The great difficulty lies in selecting the most appropriate soup for each particular occasion; it would be well to first select your bill of fare, after which decide upon the soup.

The season, and force of circumstances, may compel you to decide upon a heavy fish, such as salmon, trout, or other oleaginous fishes, and heavy joints and entrées.

Under these circumstances it must necessarily follow that a light soup should begin the dinner, and *vice versa*; for large parties, one light and one heavy soup is always in order.

Okra, as in Okroshka, is a tasty, underutilized vegetable in good soups and stews - Image: Leonid Dzhepko

There is as much art in arranging a bill of fare and harmonizing the peculiarities of the various dishes, as there is in preparing the colors for a painting; the soup represents the pivot upon which harmony depends.

Soups may be divided into four classes: clear, thick, purées or bisques, and chowders. A purée is made by rubbing the cooked ingredients through a fine sieve; an ordinary thick soup is made by adding various thickening ingredients to the soup stock; clear soups are, properly speaking, the juices of meats, served in a convenient and appetizing form.

Chowders are quite distinct from the foregoing, being compounds of an infinite variety of fish, flesh, fowl, or vegetables, in proportions to suit the fluctuating ideas of the cook; the object sought is to prepare a thick, highly seasoned compound, without reducing the ingredients to the consistency of a purée.

It is impossible to have good soup without a sufficiency of good meat; thoroughly boiled, carefully skimmed, and moderately seasoned. Meat that is too bad for anything else is too bad for soup. Cold meat recooked, adds little to its taste or nourishment, and it is in vain to attempt to give poor soup a factitious flavor by the disguise of strong spices, or other substances which are disagreeable or unpalatable to at least one half the eaters, and frequently unwholesome. Rice and barley add to the insipidity of weak soups, having no taste of their own. And even if the meat is good, too large a proportion of water, and too small a quantity of animal substance will render it flat and vapid.

Every family has, or ought to have, some personal knowledge of certain poor people—people to whom their broken victuals would be acceptable. Let then the most of their cold, fresh meat be set apart for those who can ill afford to buy meat in market. To them it will be an important acquisition; while those who indulge in fine clothes, fine furniture, &c., had best be consistent, and allow themselves the nourishment and enjoyment of freshly cooked food for each meal. Therefore where there is no absolute necessity of doing otherwise, let the soup always be made of meat bought expressly for the purpose, and of one sort only, except when the flavor is to be improved by the introduction of ham.

In plain cooking, every dish should have a distinct taste of its natural flavor predominating. Let the soup, for instance, be of beef, mutton, or veal, but not of all three; and a chicken, being overpowered by the meat, adds nothing to the general flavor.

Soup meat that has been boiled long enough to extract the juices thoroughly, becomes too tasteless to furnish, afterwards, a good dish for the table; with the exception of mutton, which may be eaten very well after it has done its duty in the soup pot, when it is much liked by many persons with simple tastes. Few who are accustomed to living at hotels, can relish hotel soups, which (even in houses where most other things are unexceptionable), is seldom such as can be approved by persons who are familiar with good tables. Hotel soups and hotel hashes, (particularly those that are dignified with French names), are notoriously made of cold scraps, leavings, and in some houses, are the absolute refuse of the kitchen. In most cases, the sight of a hotel stock pot would cause those who saw it, to forego soup forever.

If the directions are exactly followed, the soups contained in the following pages will be found palatable, nutritious, and easily made; but they require plenty of good ingredients, with no compromise made either in stringy meats or vegetables past their best.

A modern slow cooker simplifies the process of cooking good soup and stews, sacrificing little of the taste - Image: MECU

All soups should be boiled slowly at first, that the essence of the meat may be thoroughly drawn forth. The lid of the pot should be kept close, unless when it is necessary to remove it for taking off the scum, which should be done frequently and carefully. If this is neglected, the scum will boil back again into the soup, spoil it, and make it impure or muddled.

When no more scum arises, and the meat is all in rags, dropping from the bones, it is time to put in the vegetables, seasoning and not till then; and if it should have boiled away too much, then is the time to add a little hot water from another kettle. Add also a large crust of bread or two. It may now be made to boil faster, and the thickening must be put in. This is a table-spoonful or more of flour mixed to a smooth paste with a little water, and enriched with a tea-spoonful of good butter, or beef-dripping. This thickening is indispensable to all soups. Let it be stirred in well. If making a rich soup that requires wine, let this be the final thing added, just before the soup is taken from the fire.

When all is quite done and thoroughly boiled, cover the bottom of a tureen with small squares of bread or toast, and dip or pour the soup into it, leaving all the bones and shreds of meat in the pot. To let any of the sediment get into the tureen is slovenly and vulgar. Not a particle of this should ever be found in a soup-plate. There are cooks who, if not prevented, will put all the refuse into the tureen; so that, when helped, the plates are half full of shreds of meat and scraps of bone, while all the best of the soup is kept back for the kitchen. Obviously as patrons of hotels or restaurants, there's rarely any way for us to ensure this hasn't been the case until the results of this poor practice sits before us in a bowl.

Soup may be colored yellow with grated carrots, red with tomato juice, and green with the juice of pounded spinach—the coloring to be stirred in after the skimming is over. These colorings are improvements both to its look and flavor. It may be browned with scorched flour, kept ready always for the purpose. Never put cloves or allspice into soup— they give it a blackish ashy dirt color, and their taste is so strong as to overpower everything else. Both these coarse spices are out of use at good tables, and none are introduced in nice cookery but mace, nutmeg, ginger, and cinnamon.

The meat boiled in soup gives out more of its essence, when cut off the bone, and divided into small pieces, always removing the fat. The bones, however, should go in, as they contain much glutinous substance, adding to the strength and thickness of the soup, which cannot be palatable or wholesome unless all the grease is carefully skimmed off.

In cold weather, good soup, if carefully covered and kept in a cool place, and boiled over again for half an hour without any additional water, will be better on the second day than on the first.

It is an excellent way in winter to boil the meat and bones on the first day, without any vegetables. Then, when very thick and rich, strain the liquid into a large pan; cover it, and set it away till next morning—it should then be found a thick jelly. Cut it in pieces, having scraped off the sediment from the bottom—then add the vegetables, and boil them in the soup.

Soup Stocks and Accompaniments

The word stock when used in cooking means the foundation or basis upon which soups and sauces depend; it is therefore the most important part of soup making. Care should be exercised that nothing in the least tainted or decayed enters the stock pot; it is very desirable that soup stock be prepared a day or two before the main soup is cooked; the seasoning should be added in moderation at first, as it is difficult to restore a soup that has been damaged by over seasoning.

A vegetable stock in progress - Image: Stacy Spensley

Milk or cream should be boiled and strained and added hot when intended for soups; when eggs are used beat them thoroughly, and add while the soup is hot. Should they be added when the soup is boiling, they are very apt to separate, and give the soup the appearance of having curdled; the best plan is to beat up the egg with a little of the warm soup, then add it to the soup gradually.

In summer, soup stock should be boiled from day to day, if kept any length of time, else it may become sour: should this happen, add a piece of charcoal to the soup, boil, cool, and strain into freshly scalded earthen or porcelain-lined ware. On no account allow the soup stock to become cold in an iron pot or saucepan.

Beef Stock

Take six pounds of soup meat, cut it up into good sized pieces, break the bones into small pieces, place them in the stock pot, and add five quarts of cold water and two ounces of salt; boil slowly for five hours, remove the scum as fast as it rises; cut up three white turnips and three carrots, add these to the soup with two stalks of celery, one large onion quartered, six cloves, teaspoonful of whole peppers, and a small bunch of herbs.

When the vegetables are thoroughly cooked, strain the soup into a large saucepan, and set it on back of range to keep hot, but not to boil, cut one pound of lean raw beef into fine pieces, put in into a saucepan, and add the whites and shells of four eggs; season with salt, pepper, and a little chopped parsley or celery tops; squeeze these together with your hand for fifteen minutes, until they are thoroughly incorporated, then add to the warm soup; allow the soup to simmer slowly one hour; taste for seasoning; strain into crocks, or serve. This is now called consommé or bouillon, and is the basis of nearly all soups; such items as macaroni, sago, Italian paste, Macedoine, and, in fact, nearly all kinds of cereals and soup ingredients may be added to this stock at different times to produce variety; they should all be boiled separately before adding to the soup.

Calf's feet and knuckle of veal may be added to the original or first pot if a very strong stock is required.

Veal Stock

Chop up three slices of bacon and two pounds of the neck of veal; place in a stew pan with a pint of water or beef stock, and simmer for half an hour; then add two quarts of stock, one onion, a carrot, a bouquet of herbs, four stalks of celery, half a teaspoonful of bruised whole peppers, and a pinch of nutmeg with a teaspoonful of salt; boil gently for two hours, removing the scum in the meantime. Strain into an earthen crock, and when cold remove the fat. A few bones of poultry added, with an additional quantity of water or stock, will improve it.

Image: Hutschi

Croutons

Cut thick slices of somewhat stale, quality or homemade bread half an inch thick. Trim off all crust and cut each slice into squares; fry these in very hot oil; drain them on a clean napkin, and add six or eight of the crispy products to each portion of soup within each respective bowl.

While dumplings are commonly associated with Oriental soups, they are infact very versatile

Marrow Dumplings for Soups

Grate the crust of a breakfast bread roll, and break the remainder into crumbs; soak these in cold milk; drain, and add two ounces of flour; chop up half a pound of beef marrow freed from skin and sinews; beat up the yolks of five eggs; mix all together thoroughly, if too moist add some of the grated crumbs; salt and pepper to taste; form into small round dumplings; boil them in the soup for half an hour before serving.

Soup glaze Aspic with meat inside - Image: Gmelfi

Soup Glaze

Glaze is made from rich soup stock, boiled down until it forms a dark, strong jelly. It is used in coloring soups and sauces and for glazing entrées. It should be kept refrigerated in a stone crock pot. This means of production also facilitates the making of Aspic, wherein meats and vegetables are encased directly within the jellied meat stock.

Soup, Stews and Broths

We commence now with our great list of soups, stews and broths.

Artichoke Soup

Melt a piece of butter the size of an egg in a saucepan; then fry in it one white turnip sliced, one red onion sliced, three pounds of artichokes washed, pared, and sliced, and a rasher of bacon.

Stir these in the boiling butter for about ten minutes, add gradually one pint of stock. Let all boil together until the vegetables are thoroughly cooked, then add three pints more of stock; stir it well; add pepper and salt to taste, strain and press the vegetables through a sieve, and add one pint of boiling milk. Boil for five minutes more and serve.

Asparagus Soup

Take seventy-five heads of asparagus; cut away the hard, tough part, and boil the rest until tender. Drain them, and throw half into cold water until the soup is nearly ready, and press the other half through a hair sieve. Stir the pressed asparagus into two pints of stock, and let it boil; add salt, pepper, and a small lump of sugar. Cut the remaining heads of asparagus into peas; put them into the soup, and in a few minutes serve. If necessary color with a little spinach green.

Beef and barley soup - Image: WindyWinters

Barley Soup

Put into a stock pot a knuckle of veal and two pounds of shoulder of mutton chopped up; cover with one gallon of cold water; season with salt, whole peppers, and a blade of mace; boil for three hours, removing the scum as fast as it rises. Boil carrots gently until soft but retaining some natural crunch.

Wash half a pint of barley in cold water, drain and cover it with milk, and let it stand for half an hour, drain and add to the soup; boil half an hour longer, moderately; strain, trim the meat from the bone, chop up a little parsley, celery tops, add a few tablespoonsful to the soup and serve.

Beef Soup bathed in Tea

Take half a pound of lean beef; cut it up into small bits; let it soak in a pint of water for three-quarters of an hour; then put both into a quart champagne bottle with just a suspicion of salt. Cork tightly, and wire the cork, so as to prevent its popping out. Set the bottle in a saucepan full of warm water, boil gently for an hour and a half, and strain through a napkin. Beef tea, without the fibrin of the meat, if administered often to a patient, will tend to weaken, instead of strengthening the invalid; always add about a teaspoonful of finely chopped raw meat to a goblet of the tea, and let it stand in the tea for about five minutes before serving.

Bisque of Crabs

Boil twelve hard-shell crabs for thirty minutes, and drain; when cold break them apart, pick out the meat carefully, scrape off all fat adhering to the upper shell, and save these for devilled crabs (an excellent recipe for devilled crabs may be found in "Salads and Sauces.")

Set the crab meat aside; put the under shell and the claws in a mortar with half a pound of butter and a cupful of cold boiled rice, and pound them as smooth as possible; then put this into a saucepan, and add a heaping teaspoonful of salt, a bouquet of assorted herbs, a dozen whole peppers, a blade of mace, and three quarts of stock; boil slowly for one hour, pour it through a sieve, and work as much of the pulp through the sieve as possible. Place the soup on the range to keep warm, but not to boil.

Beat up the yolk of one egg, and add it slowly to a quart of warm milk previously boiled; whisk the milk into the soup; taste for seasoning. Now take the crab meat and heat it in a little boiling water, drain, put it into a hot soup tureen, pour the soup over it and serve.

Image: Stuart Spivack

Bisque of Lobster

Procure two large live lobsters; chop them up while raw, shells and all; put them into a mortar with three-fourths of a pound of butter, three raw eggs, and one quarter of a pound of cold boiled rice: pound to a paste, moisten with a little water or stock, then set aside. Fry out two slices of bacon fat, add to it one minced onion, a tablespoonful of chopped celery tops, one chopped long red pepper, one sliced carrot, and a quart of stock, boil and pour the whole into a saucepan. Add the lobster and three pints more of stock; boil slowly for two hours; strain, and rub the ingredients through a sieve. Return to the soup; keep it warm, but do not allow it to boil. If too thick, add a little more stock; add salt to taste. Boil one quart of cream; whisk it into the soup; taste again for seasoning; pour it into a hot soup tureen, and send to table.

This soup can be prepared by following receipt for bisque of crab, or it may be prepared by adding boiled lobster to a strong veal stock, and colored red by pounding the coral with butter, and adding this to the soup.

Bouille-abaisse

Take six pounds of cod-fish; cut it up into small pieces; chop two red onions; put them in a stew pan with an ounce of butter; let them brown without burning. Now add the fish and four tablespoonfuls of fine olive-oil, a bruised clove of garlic, two bay leaves, four slices of lemon peeled and quartered, half a pint of Shrewsbury tomato catsup, and half a salt-spoonful of saffron. Add sufficient hot soup stock to cover the whole; boil slowly for half to three-quarters of an hour; skim carefully while boiling; when ready to serve add a tablespoonful of chopped celery tops.

Cauliflower Soup

Fry half an onion in a very little butter; when it is a light brown add a tablespoonful of minced raw ham and two or three stalks of celery, then add a quart of soup stock; simmer slowly for half an hour. Boil for twenty-five or thirty minutes one medium-sized head of cauliflower in water slightly salted.

Strain the contents of the frying-pan into a saucepan, and add one quart more of stock. Drain the cauliflower; rub it through a fine sieve into the stock; boil just once; draw to one side of the fire; taste for seasoning. Now dissolve a teaspoonful of rice flour in half a cupful of cold milk; whisk the soup thoroughly; pour into a hot tureen, and serve.

Chestnut soup with garnish - Image: Edsel Little

Chestnut Soup

Remove the outer peel or coating from twenty-five quality chestnuts; pour scalding water over them, and rub off the inner coating. Put them into a saucepan with one quart of soup stock, and boil for three-quarters of an hours; drain; rub them through a colander, then through a sieve, with one tablespoonful of cracker dust, or pound to a paste in a mortar; season with salt and pepper; add gradually the stock in which they were boiled; add one pint more of stock; boil once, and draw to one side of the fire.

Beat up the yolks of two raw eggs; add them to one quart of warm milk; whisk the milk into the soup; taste for seasoning; pour into a hot tureen, and send to table with croutons.

Chicken Broth for the Infirm

This soup is ideal for those suffering from illness, or the elderly requiring a nutritious but easily digested meal.

Procure a dry-picked roasting chicken; cut it in halves; put one half in the ice box; chop the other half into neat pieces; put it into a small saucepan; add one quart of cold water, a little salt and a leaf of celery; simmer gently for two hours; remove the oily particles thoroughly; strain the broth into a bowl; when cooled a little, serve to the convalescent. Serve the meat with the broth.

Chicken soup - Image: Deborah Austin

Chicken Soup

Take three young male chickens; cut them up; put them in a saucepan with three quarts of veal stock. (A sliced carrot, one turnip, and one head of celery may be put with them and removed before the soup is thickened.) Let them simmer for an hour. Remove all the white flesh; return the rest of the birds to the soup, and boil gently for two hours.

Pour a little of the liquid over a quarter of a pound of bread crumbs, and when they are well soaked put it in a mortar with the white flesh of the birds, and pound the whole to a smooth paste: add a pinch of ground mace, salt, and a little cayenne pepper; press the mixture through a sieve, and boil once more, adding a pint of boiling cream; thicken with a little flour mixed in cold milk; remove the bones, and serve.

Chicken Soup, No. 2

Cut up one chicken, put into a stew pan two quarts of cold water, a teaspoonful of salt, and one pod of red pepper; when half-done add two desert spoonfuls of well washed rice: when thoroughly cooked, remove the bird from the soup, tear a part of the breast into shreds (saving the remainder of the fowl for a salad), and add it to the soup with a wine-glass full of cream.

Giblet Stew

An economical, and at the same time excellent, stew, is made from the legs, neck, heart, wings, and gizzard of all kinds of poultry. These odds and ends are usually plentiful during the holiday season.

To turn them to account, follow general instructions for chicken soup; add a little rice, and your soup is complete.

Clam Broth

Procure three dozen little-neck clams in the shell; wash them well in cold water; put them in a saucepan, cover with a quart of hot water; boil fifteen minutes; drain; remove the shells; chop up the clams, and add them to the hot broth with a pat of butter; salt if necessary and add a little cayenne; boil ten minutes, pour into a soup tureen, add a slice of toast, and send to table. This is the mode adopted when we do not have a clam opener in the house.

Raw, freshly opened clams should be chopped fine and prepared in the manner above described. The large clams are better for chowders than for stews and broth.

Clam chowder - Image: Ron Dollete

Clam Chowder

Chop up fifty large clams; cut eight medium-sized potatoes into small square pieces, and keep them in cold water until wanted.

Chop one large, red onion fine, and cut up half a pound of larding pork into small pieces.

Procure an good saucepan, and see that it is very clean and free from rust; set it on the range, and when very hot, throw the pieces of pork into it, fry them brown; next add the onion, and fry it brown; add one fourth of the chopped clams, then one fourth of the chopped potato, and two pilot crackers quartered, a teaspoonful of salt, one chopped, long, red pepper, a teaspoonful of powdered thyme and half a pint of canned tomato pulp.

Repeat this process until the clams and potato are used, omitting the seasoning; add hot water enough to cover all, simmer slowly three hours. Should it become too thick, add more hot water; occasionally remove the pot from the range, take hold of the handle, and twist the pot round several times; this is done to prevent the chowder from burning. On no account disturb the chowder with a spoon or ladle until done; now taste for seasoning, as it is much easier to season properly after the chowder is cooked than before. A few celery tops may be added if desired.

Simple consommé - Image: Rainer Zenz

Consommé

This is nothing more than beef stock, with a little more attention given to clarifying it. It is always acceptable if the dinner to follow is composed of heavy joints and side dishes. If the party consists of more than twenty, serve one thick soup and one light soup or consommé.

Consommé Colbert

Prepare a strong consommé; add to two quarts of it a tablespoonful each of shredded young turnips and carrots and a tablespoonful of green peas; simmer until the vegetables are tender; taste for seasoning.

Poach four eggs in hot water in the usual manner; send these to table with the soup. In serving add one poached egg to each plate. It is well always to poach two extra eggs to be used should any of the others be broken in the service.

Cream Soup

Prepare two quarts of strong veal stock; set it on the back part of the range to simmer.

Boil one quart of cream; whisk it into the stock; pour it into a hot tureen, and serve with croutons. If convenient the breast of a boiled chicken may be added.

Seafood and fish chowder - Image: Benreis

Fish Chowder

Take two fine, fresh cod-fish, weighing six pounds each; clean them well; cut the fish lengthwise from the bone, and cut it into pieces two inches square. Chop up the bones and heads; put them into a saucepan; add three quarts of warm water, one red onion sliced, heaping teaspoonful of salt, a dozen bruised peppercorns, and a few stalks of celery. Boil until the fish drops from the bones; then strain into another saucepan.

Cut into small squares one peck of small potatoes and a pound and a half of salt pork; arrange the fish, pork, and potatoes into mounds; divide each equally into four parts; add one quarter of the fish to the stock, next a quarter of the pork, then a quarter of the potato, and three pilot crackers, broken into quarters, salt, pepper, and a little thyme. Repeat this process until the remaining three quarters of pork, fish, and potato, are used; cover all with warm milk; simmer slowly until the fish is tender, care being taken that the soup does not boil over; now taste for seasoning, serve as neatly as possible.

The above is the old-fashioned New England fish chowder. Clams may be used instead of fish.

German Soup

Melt half an ounce of fresh butter in a saucepan; when very hot, add half an onion, chopped fine, and a teaspoonful of caraway seeds. When the onion is slightly browned, add three quarts of strong veal stock, well-seasoned; simmer gently for three quarters of an hour. Prepare some marrow dumplings; boil them in water, or a portion of the soup, and serve.

Green Turtle Soup

Many housewives imagine that green turtle is too expensive, and too difficult to prepare for household use, and for these reasons it is seldom met with in private families, except in tin cans from far eastern stores. Even this is not always made from turtle, with substitutes such as squid or crab common.

This soup is not any more expensive than many other kinds. A pound of turtle meat can be purchased in Oriental supermarkets, with the price varying by locality according to the law of supply and demand. The only objection to small turtles is that they do not contain a very large percentage of the green fat, which is nutritious and as such valued.

Procure some turtle meat and allow it to drain and cool over night; next morning place it on the working table, lay it on its back, and make an incision round the inner edge of the shell; then remove it. Now remove the intestines carefully, and be very careful that you do not break the gall; throw these away; cut off the fins and all fleshy particles, and set them aside; trim out the fat, which has a bluish tint when raw; wash it well in several waters. Chop up the upper and under shells with a cleaver; put them with the fins into a large saucepan; cover them with boiling water; let stand ten minutes; drain and rub off the horny, scaly particles, with a kitchen towel.

Scald a large saucepan, and put all the meat and shell into it (except the fat); cover with hot water; add a little salt, and boil four hours. Skim carefully, and drain; put the meat into a large crock; remove the bones, and boil the fat in the stock. This does not take very long if first scalded. When done, add it also to the crock; pour the stock into another crock; let it cool, and remove all scum and oily particles; this is quite work enough for one day. Clean the saucepans used, and dry them thoroughly.

Next day fry out half a pound of fat ham; then add one chopped onion, one bay leaf, six cloves, one blade of mace, two tablespoonfuls of chopped celery tops, a tablespoonful of salt, a teaspoonful of white pepper, and one quart of ordinary soup stock. Simmer for half an hour. Now put the turtle stock on the fire; when hot strain the seasoning into it; remove the turtle from the other crock, cut it up, and add to the stock; now add a pint of dry sherry.

Do not let the soup come to a boil; taste for seasoning, and if herbs are needed tie a string to a bunch of mixed herbs, throw them into the soup, and tie the other end to the saucepan handle; taste often, and when palatable, remove the herbs. If the soup is not dark enough, brown a very little flour and add to it. Keep the soup quite hot until served; add quartered slices of lemon and the yolk of a hardboiled egg, quartered just before serving; send to table with a decanter of sherry.

The yolks of the eggs may be worked to a paste, and made into round balls to imitate turtle eggs if this is desired.

I have placed before my readers this complicated recipe in as simple a form as it is possible to do, having carefully avoided all the technical formulas used in the profession.

Seafood Gumbo - Image: Gary Stevens

Gumbo Soup

Cut up two chickens, two slices of ham, and two onions into dice; flour them, and fry the whole to a light brown; then fill the frying pan with boiling water; stir it a few minutes, and turn the whole into a saucepan containing three quarts of boiling water. Let it boil for forty minutes, removing the scum.

In the meantime soak three pints of okra in cold water for twenty minutes; cut them into thin slices, and add to the other ingredients; let it boil for one hour and a half. Add a quart of canned tomatoes and a cupful of boiled rice half an hour before serving.

Note that there are many different local varieties of Gumbo, using beef or seafood respectively, making this dish quite versatile. The image appended depicts a Gumbo prepared in the Caribbean style with large shrimp.

Julienne Soup

Cut into fine shreds, an inch long, two carrots, two turnips, two heads of celery, and the white ends of two spring leeks. Put them into a frying pan, with one ounce of butter, a teaspoonful of salt, and one lump of cut sugar; simmer until tender, then add a cupful of stock. Put two quarts of veal stock in a saucepan; add the vegetables, and a teaspoonful of chopped parsley, a little fresh sorrel if convenient (wild wood sorrel is the best for julienne) shredded. Taste for seasoning; boil once, and serve.

Lentil Soup

Lentils are very nutritious, and form the basis of a most excellent soup; but they are little used in American cookery. Soak a pint of dry lentils for two hours; put them in a saucepan; add two quarts of cold water, half an onion, two or three celery tops, salt, whole peppers, and two or three ounces of the small end of a ham. Boil gently for three hours; add a little more hot water, if the quantity has been reduced by boiling, pour through a sieve, remove the ham, onion and celery; rub the lentils through a sieve, return to the soup; whisk it thoroughly; taste for seasoning, and serve with croutons.

Liebig's Soup

An excellent soup may be prepared at short notice, as follows:—Take half an onion, three or four outer stocks of celery, one carrot sliced, salt, pepper, and a very little mace. Boil these in two quarts of water for half an hour; strain, and add to the water two tablespoonfuls of Liebig's Extract of meat; whisk thoroughly, taste for seasoning, and serve.

Macaroni Soup

Boil half a pound of Macaroni for half an hour, in three pints of water slightly salted; add a blade of mace. When done, drain, and cut it into two inch pieces. Put three pints of soup stock into a saucepan; add the macaroni; taste for seasoning, boil a moment and serve.

Mock Turtle Soup

Take half a calf's head, with the skin on; remove the brains. Wash the head in several waters, and let it soak in cold water for an hour. Put it in a saucepan with five quarts of beef stock; let it simmer gently for an hour; remove the scum carefully. Take up the head and let it get cold; cut the meat from the bones into pieces an inch square, and set them in the ice-box.

Dissolve two ounces of butter in a frying pan; mince a large onion, and fry it in the butter until nicely browned, and add to the stock in which the head was cooked. Return the bones to the stock; simmer the soup, removing the scum until no more rises. Put in a carrot, a turnip, a bunch of parsley, a bouquet of herbs, a dozen outer stalks of celery, two blades of mace and the rind of one lemon, grated; salt and pepper to taste.

Boil gently for two hours, and strain the soup through a cloth. Mix three ounces of browned flour with a pint of the soup; let simmer until it thickens, then add it to the soup. Take the pieces of head out of the ice-box, and add to the soup; let them simmer until quite tender. "Before serving add a little Worcestershire sauce, a tablespoonful of anchovy paste, a glass of port or sherry, and two lemons sliced, each slice quartered, with the rind trimmed off." Warm the wine a very little before adding it to the soup. Keep in ice-box three or four days before using. Serve the brains as a side dish.

Mulligatawny Soup - Image: Miansari66

Mulligatawny Soup

Divide a large chicken into neat pieces; take a knuckle of veal, and chop it up; put all into a large saucepan, and add one gallon of water; salt; boil for three hours or until reduced one-third. Put an ounce of butter in a hot frying pan, cut up two red onions, and fry them in the butter.

Into a half pint of the stock put two heaping tablespoonfuls of curry powder; add this to the onion, then add the whole to the soup, now taste for seasoning. Some like a little wine, but these are the exception and not the rule. Before serving add half a slice of lemon to each portion. Many prefer a quantity of rice to be added to the soup before it is finished; the rice should be first well washed and parboiled.

Mutton Broth

Take four pounds of lean mutton trimmings; cut them into neat pieces; put them into a saucepan; add three quarts of cold water, one heaping teaspoonful of salt. Bruise, and add six peppercorns, three or four celery tops, and one young leek. Boil slowly for two hours; remove the scum as it rises. Boil a cupful of rice for twenty minutes; add it to the soup, and taste for seasoning; remove the celery, leek, and mutton bones; pour the soup into a hot tureen, and serve.

Substitute a knuckle of veal for mutton, and you will have an excellent veal broth.

Onion Soup

Peel and cut into small pieces three medium-sized onions; fry them in a little butter until tender, but not brown; pour over them a pint of stock; add a little salt and cayenne. Simmer for fifteen minutes; press the soup through a sieve; put it in a saucepan, and add three tablespoonfuls of grated bread crumbs, and half a cup of hot cream. Taste for seasoning, and serve with small slices of toast.

Oxtail Soup

Take two oxtails; cut them into joints, and cut each joint into four pieces; put them into a pan with two ounces of butter, and fry them for ten minutes. Slice two onions, one turnip, two carrots, and a dozen outer stalks of celery, and fry in the same butter, with three slices of bacon cut up fine; fry to a light brown. Turn the ingredients into a saucepan with a quart of stock or ham water, and boil quickly for half an hour, then add two more quarts of stock, a bouquet of herbs, two bay-leaves, a dozen whole peppers crushed, a few cloves, and salt to taste. Simmer until the meat is quite tender; then take it out; strain the soup; skim off the fat, and thicken with two ounces of flour. Return the meat to the soup; add a tablespoonful of Worcestershire, and a cupful of sherry, and serve with grated rusks.

Oyster Soup

Wet a saucepan with cold water; pour into it two quarts of milk. When at boiling point, add two dozen oysters and a pint of oyster liquor well-seasoned with salt and pepper. Dissolve a tablespoonful of rice flour in a little cold milk; finally add a large tablespoonful of table butter; do not let the soup boil again as it will contract the oysters. Pour into a tureen, taste for salting, and serve, a few broken crackers may be added. The object in wetting the pan is to prevent the milk from burning.

Image: Beck

Pea and Ham Soup

Cut two large slices of ham into dice, with a sliced onion, and fry them in a little bacon fat until they are lightly browned. Cut up one turnip, one large carrot, four outer stalks of celery, and one leek into small pieces; add these last ingredients to the ham and onion, and let them simmer for fifteen minutes; then pour over them three quarts of corned-beef water or hot water, and add a pint of split peas which have been soaked in cold water over night.

Boil gently until the peas are quite tender stirring constantly to prevent burning; then add salt and pepper to taste, and a teaspoonful of brown sugar. Remove the soup from the fire, and rub through a sieve; if it is not thick enough to suit your taste, add a few ounces of flour mixed smoothly in a little cold milk; return the soup to the fire, and simmer for half an hour. Cut up four slices of American bread into small dice, and fry the pieces in very hot fat until nicely browned; place them on a napkin or towel, and add a few to each plate or tureen of soup just before it goes to table.

Pea Soup - Economical version

This simpler version of pea soup is perfect on the fly or in a pinch.

Boil for four hours two quarts of green pea hulls in four quarts of water, in which beef, mutton, or fowl has been boiled, then add a bunch or bouquet of herbs, salt and pepper, a teaspoonful of butter, and a quart of milk. Rub through a hair sieve, thicken with a little flour, and serve with croutons, as in the previous recipe.

Potato Soup

Wash and peel two dozen small sized potatoes; put them into a saucepan with two onions; add three quarts of corned-beef water; boil for one hour and a half until the potatoes fall to pieces. Pour the soup through a sieve, and rub the potato through it to a fine pulp; put the whole into the saucepan again; when very hot add a pint of hot rich cream, salt and pepper, if necessary; whisk thoroughly; pour into a tureen, add croutons, and serve.

Purée of Beans

Soak two quarts of small, white beans overnight; change the water twice; drain, put them into a pot or saucepan, and cover them with cold water. Boil slowly for six hours; as the water evaporates, add hot water. One hour before the beans are cooked add one pound of salt pork, a bunch of fresh herbs, half a dozen whole cloves, salt if necessary; when done pour the soup through a sieve, remove the pork and seasoning, and rub the soup through a sieve; add the pulp to the stock; taste for seasoning; pour the soup into a tureen, add croutons and serve. Many prefer a ham bone to pork.

Purée of Clams

Chop twenty-five large hard-shell clams, very fine, and put them aside; fry half a chopped red onion in an ounce of hot butter; add a teaspoonful of chopped celery tops, a blade of mace, one salted anchovy, six whole peppers, and a pint of soup stock. Let it boil; then strain into a saucepan; add the chopped clams and one quart of stock or hot water.

Boil slowly one hour; strain all the clams through a sieve twice, and return to the stock; season with salt and cayenne. Keep the soup warm, but do not let it boil again; taste for seasoning. Boil one pint of cream in a saucepan previously wet with cold water; strain it, and add to the soup slowly. Mix a teaspoonful of rice flour in a little cold milk; add to the soup; whisk the soup; taste again for seasoning; pour it into a hot tureen, and serve.

A plainer form of rabbit stew prepared in Sardinia - Image: Heather Cowper

Rabbit Stew

Cut up two jack rabbits into neat pieces; put them into a stew pan containing one quarter of a pound of melted butter; add a slice of fat bacon cut into small pieces. Fry for five minutes in the butter; slice two small carrots, and two red onions, and add to the saucepan with one bay leaf, one blade of mace, four cloves, a few green celery stalks, one ounce of salt, and one long red pepper.

Pour over all, one gallon of stock; simmer gently for nearly three hours; skim carefully; strain into a saucepan, and set on back of range to keep hot, but not to boil. Add half a pint of dry sherry, and serve with croutons. If not dark enough add a little glaze.

Scotch Broth

Take two pounds of mutton trimmings; cut into neat pieces; put into a saucepan with three quarts of water, one large red onion, salt, and a dozen whole peppers. Boil gently, and remove the scum as it rises; wash half a pint of barley; soak it while the soup is boiling, and add it at the end of the first hour. Let the soup boil for two hours longer; taste for seasoning; pour slowly into a soup tureen, leaving the meat in the saucepan. Some prefer to take the meat out of the soup, and after removing the bones they return the meat to the soup.

Sorrel Soup

Sorrel is an excellent ingredient for soup. Its acid leaves are much appreciated by the French; the wild sorrel may be used, but now that truck gardeners are cultivating it extensively, it will be found less troublesome to use the latter.

The Germans make the best sorrel soup; their recipe is as follows:—Wash and pick over two quarts of sorrel; remove the stems; then cut the sorrel into pieces. Heat two ounces of butter in a small saucepan; add the sorrel and a few blades of chives; cover without water and allow it to steam for half an hour. Stir to prevent burning; sprinkle over this a tablespoonful of flour free from lumps. Now add three quarts of well-seasoned veal stock; taste for seasoning; boil once, and send to table with croutons or small bits of toast. This an excellent spring and summer soup.

Spring Soup

Take two quarts of nicely seasoned veal stock; place it on the range to keep hot, but not to boil. Cut into neat strips four young carrots, four young spring turnips, and two spring leeks; add them to the stock. Now add half a pint of fresh green peas; boil gently for fifteen minutes; taste for seasoning, and serve.

Turkey Soup

Take the remains of a cold roast turkey, trim off all the meat, break up the bones, and put them into a saucepan; cover them with two quarts of veal stock; salt and cayenne to taste. Boil gently for one hour; strain and skim. Now add the flesh of the turkey; simmer gently; dissolve a tablespoonful of rice flour in a little cold milk, and add it to the soup. Let it come to a boil; taste for seasoning, and serve with croutons.

Vegetable Soup

Wash and clean two carrots and two turnips; cut them into slices, and cut each slice into small narrow strips; put them into a saucepan with four stalks of celery cut into inch pieces, a dozen button onions, one long red pepper, and a teaspoonful of salt; add three quarts of soup stock; boil until the vegetables are tender, add a lump of sugar, and serve. The carrots and turnips may be cut into fancy shapes with a vegetable cutter.

Oyster vermicelli soup - Image: Prattflora

Vermicelli Soup

Take one quarter of a pound of vermicelli; break it into pieces, and boil it for five minutes; drain and add it to three pints of strong soup stock. Boil once; draw to one side, and simmer gently for twenty minutes. Should any scum arise, remove it; taste for seasoning, and send to table with a little Parmesan cheese.

This soup is also well-accompanied by seafood, particularly oysters. Seasonings may also be elaborated upon with black pepper and fresh coriander.

Image: Stuart Spivack

Cream of Asparagus

Wash one bundle of asparagus, cut off the tips and throw them into a pint of boiling water, add a teaspoonful of salt, and simmer gently for fifteen minutes. Strain them and save the water; to this water add the remaining part of the bundle, cut into small pieces. Cook fifteen minutes and press through a colander. Put one quart of milk into a double boiler; rub together two tablespoonfuls of butter and two tablespoonfuls of flour. Add a little of the hot milk to this and work until perfectly smooth, then stir into the milk and cook five minutes. Heat the asparagus mixture, turn the milk quickly into it, season, add the asparagus tips, and serve. This cannot be boiled or it will curdle.

Cream of Celery

Cut up six stalks of celery into half-inch pieces; put them into a saucepan with one red onion quartered, one blade of mace, salt, and a few whole peppers; add a quart of veal stock, and boil for one hour. Rub the ingredients through a sieve; put the pulp into a saucepan, and add one quart more of veal stock; boil; then draw to one side of fire to keep hot.

Boil three pints of cream; strain it into the soup; whisk the soup at the same time (if not thick enough to suit your taste add a little flour); taste for seasoning; pour it into a hot tureen; serve with small pieces of toast or croutons.

Cream of Corn

Score each row of grains on six ears of sweet corn; then, with the back of the knife press it out carefully and throw the cobs into a kettle; cover with a quart of water, bring to boiling point and strain. Now, add the scraped corn to the water. Rub together two tablespoonfuls of butter and one of flour. Stir it into this corn mixture and bring to boiling point, then add one pint of hot milk; season and serve.

Cream of Chestnut

Shell and blanch one pound of large chestnuts. Cover them with a quart of boiling water; add a slice of onion, piece of celery chopped, a bay leaf, sprig of parsley and a dash of paprika. Cover and boil thirty minutes. Press first through a colander; then add one pint of milk; return the whole to the fire. Rub together two tablespoonfuls of butter and two of flour; add to the soup; cook a minute; add a palatable seasoning of salt, and then press the whole through a purée sieve. Make hot and serve with croutons.

Cream of Lettuce

Wash and pull apart two good-sized heads of lettuce. Throw them into a hot saucepan, shake over the fire until the lettuce leaves simply melt. Sprinkle over a teaspoonful of salt, then press through a sieve. Put one quart of milk in a double boiler. Rub together two tablespoonfuls of butter and two of flour, add it to the milk and stir until it thickens. Chop sufficient parsley to make two tablespoonfuls and pound it in a mortar. Put this in a bowl; mix it with the lettuce that has been pressed through the sieve. Stir in the milk, then add a half teaspoonful of beef extract, dissolved in a little of the hot milk; season and serve.

Cream of Beetroot

Take four cold, boiled beets and grate them. Dissolve a teaspoonful of beef extract in one pint of boiling water. Add it to the beets, and when they reach the boiling point add one pint of hot milk; stir in a tablespoonful of butter, palatable seasoning of salt, and when it reaches the boiling point, add tablespoonful of arrow-root dissolved in two tablespoonfuls of cold water. Bring to boiling point again, and serve.

Cream of Rice

Wash thoroughly a half pound of rice; pick out all imperfect or colored grains; put it into a saucepan and add two quarts of stock. Boil slowly for one hour; then rub the rice through a sieve twice; return it to the stock; season with salt and pepper. Care must be exercised that the rice does not adhere to the bottom of the saucepan. Simmer until wanted. Beat up the yolks of two eggs; add them slowly to a quart of warm, milk previously boiled; whisk the milk into the soup, which must not be very hot; then pour it into a hot tureen, and serve.

Pearl Sago in an Indian marketplace - Image: Parvathisri

Clear Tomato with Sago

Put one pint of stewed tomato into a saucepan, add slice of onions, bay leaf and sprig of parsley. Simmer ten minutes. Cover four tablespoonfuls of pearl sago with a pint of cold water and soak for twenty minutes. Now, stand this over the back part of the stove until the sago is perfectly clear, and the water almost boiling hot. Add to the tomatoes one pint of boiling water and two tablespoonfuls of butter, then press through a sieve. Return to the heat; add a teaspoonful of salt, half teaspoonful of pepper and then the sago. Serve at once. This soup may be varied by adding, instead of the pint of water to the tomatoes, a pint of stock.

Brown Broth

Boil and cut into dice one young carrot, one onion and one potato. Put two ounces of butter in the frying-pan, throw in the vegetables and stir carefully until they are a golden brown.

Then skim them out and put them in a saucepan. Cover with one quart of boiling water, add a bay leaf and simmer gently twenty minutes. Press through a purée sieve, return these to the kettle, add a teaspoonful of kitchen bouquet and palatable seasoning of salt and pepper. Serve with cheese balls.

Cheese Balls

Put a tablespoonful of butter and a quarter of a cup of water over the fire to boil. Stir in quickly a quarter of a cup of flour and stir for a minute. Take from the fire and add one well-beaten egg and two tablespoonfuls of grated cheese.

Drop this mixture into a greased baking pan, and bake in a quick oven fifteen minutes. The paste should not be larger than a good sized bean as you drop it on the pan. A very good way to make them is to put this mixture in a pastry bag and press it through a plain tube, and cut it off into small balls.

Image: Rootology

Bisque of Clam

Drain fifty small clams. Bring the liquor to boiling point and skim. Chop the clams fine, add them to the liquor and cook gently for ten minutes. Gently boil some sweetcorn, and set aside. Then press through a sieve. Put one quart of milk into a double boiler; add to it a bay leaf. Rub together two tablespoonfuls of butter and two of flour, and stir carefully into the milk. Cook slowly until it thickens. Now, add a teaspoonful of onion juice or grated onion, and turn in the clam mixture, and add the sweetcorn. Stir carefully for a moment, season with salt and pepper, and serve.

Remember this must not be boiled after the clam has been added to the milk. If you have white stock in the house the soup is greatly improved by having instead one quart of milk, one pint of milk and a pint of stock.

Club Clam Soup

Drain fifty small clams, then chop them fine. Mix the liquor and the clams, and add one quart of cold water, about two tablespoonfuls of chopped ham, one large onion sliced thin, quarter of a teaspoonful of mace and a sprig of parsley. Bring this slowly to a boiling point. Rub together two tablespoonfuls of butter and two of flour. Stir them into the soup carefully; add just a dash of salt and a quarter teaspoonful of pepper. Bring to boiling point, then take from the fire and turn in one pint of hot milk, to which you have just added the well-beaten yolks of four eggs. Stir quickly and serve with squares of toasted bread.

Mock Oyster Soup

Select about one dozen roots of salsify. Scrape them and throw at once into cold water to prevent discoloration. Cut the salsify crosswise into thin slices. Put them into one quart of cold water and add about two ounces of codfish. This is best in one solid piece. Simmer gently for thirty minutes and remove the codfish. Have ready one pint of milk heated in a double boiler. Add it to the salsify, then stir in carefully one tablespoonful of butter and two of flour that have been rubbed to a smooth paste. Season with salt and pepper. Then, just as you take it from the fire, add another teaspoonful of butter, cut into pieces, and it is ready to serve.

Cucumber Tapioca Soup

Boil three good-sized cucumbers, cut them into slices and cover them with one quart of white stock. Simmer gently for twenty minutes. Then press through a sieve. Soak two tablespoonfuls of pearl tapioca in one pint of milk in a cold place for one hour. Stand this in a double boiler and heat slowly until the tapioca is perfectly clear. Heat the cucumber mixture; add a teaspoonful of salt, teaspoonful of onion juice and quarter teaspoonful of pepper. Turn into the hot milk. Have ready in the tureen the yolks of two eggs, well-beaten. Pour the soup over gradually.

Quick Clear Soup

Put one pound of finely-chopped meat into one pint of cold water, beat it for about a minute with an egg beater, and let it stand for thirty minutes, while you prepare the flavoring. Stir one tablespoonful of beef extract into a quart of boiling water. Add a tablespoonful of grated onion and one bay leaf. Now bring the meat to boiling point.

Strain in a colander. Beat the white and shell of one egg with two tablespoonfuls of cold water. Put the soup you have strained from the meat over the fire, and when boiling add to the egg mixture, bring to boiling point and strain through two thicknesses of cheese cloth. Then add this to the beef extract mixture, season with teaspoonful of salt and quarter teaspoonful of pepper, and it is ready to serve.

This may be served with two tablespoonfuls of boiled rice or boiled macaroni, or with fresh rings of cucumbers. To prepare these rings cut a large cucumber into slices crosswise. With a round cutter stamp them out just as much as you can to remove the skin, and then with a smaller cutter stamp out the seeds. Throw these rings into boiling salted water and boil for twenty minutes; strain and put in the soup. Or this soup may be served à la Royal.

A La Royal

Beat two eggs until well mixed; add two tablespoonfuls of stock, half teaspoonful of salt and a quarter teaspoonful of pepper. Now add two tablespoonfuls of milk or cream, and turn into a small buttered basin or mold. Stand this mold in a pan of boiling water and cook gently, either in the oven or on the top of the stove, until the custard is "set." When cold cut into blocks or into fancy shapes. Put this in the tureen and pour over the soup.

Bisque of Salmon

Wash well a half cup of rice. Put it into a quart of water and boil rapidly for thirty minutes. Then press it through a purée sieve and add to it the salmon from a one pound can, removing first all the bones, skin and oil. Now press this again through a sieve; add a teaspoonful of salt, bay leaf, tablespoonful of grated onion and half teaspoonful of pepper.

Stand it over the back part of the stove until it is steaming hot. Heat one quart of milk in a double boiler. Rub together two tablespoonfuls of butter and two of flour. Stir this carefully into the milk and stir until perfectly smooth and thick. Then add a level teaspoonful of salt; turn this mixture into the other, remove the bay leaf, bring to scalding point, and serve. If you like this soup a little deeper color, add a few drops of cochineal. Halibut may be used in precisely the same way, of course, keeping the soup perfectly white.

Currant Soup

This soup may be made from any sort of fresh, tart fruit. It should be served for lunch perfectly cold, in either punch or bouillon cups. Put one pint of currants and one pint of water over the fire and bring to scald-point. Add half a cup of sugar. Press through a purée sieve, return to the fire and add one tablespoonful of arrow-root, moistened in two tablespoonfuls of water. Bring to boiling point until the soup is clear, then stand away to cool. If you use wine, add two tablespoonfuls of white wine. Cherries, cranberries and strawberries may be used in the same way, adding more or less sugar, according to the kind of fruit, but these soups should not be sweet. Use just enough sugar to make them palatable.

Chocolate Soup

Put three tablespoonfuls of cocoa into a double boiler, and add gradually one pint of boiling water. Stir for at least five minutes over the fire. Add four tablespoonfuls of sugar, take from the fire and add a teaspoonful of vanilla. Turn this into one pint of cracked ice, and when the soup is cold, turn into the serving cups, and put on the surface a tablespoonful of whipped cream, and serve.

Pistachio Soup

Wash one quart of nice spinach. Pick each leaf from the stem and throw into a saucepan; stand over the fire for a moment, shaking so that the spinach will not discolor. Sprinkle over a teaspoonful of salt. As soon as the spinach begins to wilt, drain and chop very fine, then pound it to a paste. Put one quart of milk into a double boiler; add one teaspoonful of almond paste unsweetened, and two ounces of pistachio nuts chopped to a powder. Cover and cook twenty minutes. Add spinach, one tablespoonful of butter, one of arrow-root, moistened, and press through a purée sieve. Add a teaspoonful of salt, dash of paprika, and serve.

Ye Gods Soup

So named for its merit befitting even the Gods, this wholesome soup is something of a classic in Northern Europe.

Peel half pound of good, fresh mushrooms; remove the lower part of stems. Wash the mushrooms, and chop them very fine with a silver knife. Put them in a saucepan, with one quart of good chicken stock. Cover and simmer gently thirty minutes; add teaspoonful of salt and simmer ten minutes longer. Put two tablespoonfuls of butter in another saucepan, add three tablespoonfuls of fine flour, mix and cook a minute without browning; add a half pint of thick cream to the mushrooms, then add the whole to the butter and flour, stir constantly until it just comes to boiling point; add dash of white pepper and serve in bouillon cups. Serve with whole wheat bread toasted in oven.

Oatmeal Soup

This unusual recipe is intended to enliven the simple dish of porridge.

Add one cup of cold cooked oatmeal to one quart of water; add a slice of onion, sprig of celery top, bay leaf, teaspoonful of salt, and a pinch of pepper. Cover and boil slowly ten minutes; add a half teaspoonful of beef extract, or, if you have stock, use it in place of water. Now press through a sieve; return to the fire; when boiling, add half pint of hot milk, and serve.

Mushroom Soup

Cut a knuckle of veal, or a neck of mutton, (or both, if they are small,) into large pieces, and remove the bones. Put it into a soup-pot with sufficient water to cover the whole, and season with a little salt and cayenne. Let it boil till the meat is in rags, skimming it well; then strain off the soup into another pot.

Have ready a large quart, or a quart and a pint of freshly-gathered mushrooms—cut them into quarters, having removed the stalks. Put them into the soup, adding a quarter of a pound (or more) of fresh butter, divided into bits and rolled in flour. Boil the whole about half an hour longer—try if the mushrooms are tender, and do not take them up till they are perfectly so. Keep the pot lid closely covered, except when you remove the lid to try the mushrooms. Lay at the bottom of the tureen a large slice of buttered toast, (cut into small squares,) and pour the soup upon it. This is a company soup.

Sweetcorn Soup

Take a knuckle of veal, and a set of calf's feet. Put them into a soup-pot with some cold boiled ham cut into pieces, and season them with pepper only. Having allowed a quart of water to each pound of meat, pour it on, and let it boil till the meat falls from the bone; strain it, and pour the liquid into a clean pot. If you live in the country, or where milk is plenty, make this soup of milk without any water.

All white soups are best of milk. You may boil in this, with the veal and feet, old chicken, (cut into pieces,) that is too tough for any other purpose. When the soup is well boiled, and the shreds all strained away, have ready (cooked by themselves in another pot) some ears of sweet corn, young and tender. Cut the grains from the cob, mix the corn with fresh butter, season it with pepper, and stir it in the strained soup. Give the whole a short boil, pour it into the tureen, and send it to table.

Venison Soup

A venison soup is excellent, made as above, with water instead of milk, and plenty of corn. And it is very convenient for a new settlement.

Tomato Soups

These five recipes cover superbly the important matter of tomato soup. We begin with the basic, meatless variety before moving onto composite types with more expensive ingredients and complex means of cooking.

Tomato soup - Image: William Stadtwald Demchick

Basic Tomato Soup

Cut six large tomatoes into small pieces. Put them into a saucepan with one pint of water, or stock, add tablespoonful of butter, slice of onion, bay leaf and a sprig of parsley. Cook slowly twenty minutes and press through a sieve sufficiently fine to remove the seeds. Return this soup to the fire, add tablespoonful of arrow root moistened in two tablespoonfuls of cold water, another tablespoonful of butter and a palatable seasoning of salt and pepper, and serve with squares of toasted bread.

Tomato Soup

Take a shin or leg of beef, and cut off all the meat. Put it, with the bones, in a large soup-pot, and season it slightly with salt and pepper. Pour on a gallon of water. Boil and skim it well. Have ready half a kilo of ripe tomatoes that have been quartered, and pressed or strained through a sieve, so as to be reduced to a pulp. Add half a dozen onions that have been sliced, and a table-spoonful of sugar to lessen a little the acid of the tomatoes. When the meat is all to rags, and the whole thoroughly done, (which will not be in less than six hours from the commencement) strain it through a colander, and thicken it a little with grated bread crumbs.

This soup will be much improved by the addition of a half peck of okras, peeled, sliced thin, and boiled with the tomatoes till quite dissolved.

Before it goes into the tureen, see that there are no shreds of meat or bits of bone left in the soup.

Tomato Soup #2

Cut four ounces of ham into dice; slice two onions, and fry with ham in two ounces of butter; when browned turn them into a saucepan containing three quarts of stock or corned-beef water, and add three carrots, two turnips, and one long red pepper, and a dozen outer stalks of celery.

Simmer gently for one hour; then add a quart of canned tomatoes; boil gently for another hour; rub the whole through a sieve, and simmer again with the liquor a few minutes; add salt, and serve with fried bread crumbs.

Family-sized Tomato Soup

Designed to serve large groups in family gatherings or general celebrations, this soup is

Take four pounds of the lean of a good piece of fresh beef. The fat is of no use for soup, as it must be skimmed off when boiling. Cut the meat in pieces, season them with a little salt and pepper, and put them into a pot with three quarts of water. The tomatoes will supply abundance of liquid. Of these you should have a large quarter of a peck.

They should be full-grown, and quite ripe. Cut each tomato into four pieces, and put them into the soup; after it has come to a boil and been skimmed. It will be greatly improved by adding a quarter of a peck of okras cut into thin round slices. Both tomatoes and okras require long and steady boiling with the meat. To lessen the extreme acid of the tomatoes, stir in a heaped table-spoonful of sugar.

Add also one large onion, peeled and minced small; and add two or three bits of fresh butter rolled in flour. The soup must boil till the meat is all to rags and the tomatoes and okras entirely dissolved, and their forms undistinguishable. Pour it off carefully from the sediment into the tureen, in the bottom of which have ready some toasted bread, cut into small squares.

Fine Tomato Soup

A premium take on the classic tomato soup, to be made with correspondingly excellent ingredients.

Take some nice fresh beef, and divest it of the bone and fat. Sprinkle it with a little salt and pepper, and pour on water, allowing to each pound of meat a pint and a half (not more) of water, and boil and skim it till it is very thick and clear, and all the essence seems to be drawn out of the meat. Scald and peel a large portion of ripe tomatoes—cut them in quarters, and laying them in a stew-pan, let them cook in their own juice till they are entirely dissolved.

When quite done, strain the tomato liquid, and stir into it a little sugar. In a third pan stew an equal quantity of sliced okras with a very little water; they must be stewed till their shape can no longer be discerned. Strain separately the meat liquor, the tomatoes, and the okras. Mix butter and flour together into a lump; knead it a little, and when all the liquids are done and strained put them into a clean soup-pan, stir in the flour and butter, and give the soup one boil up. Transfer it to your tureen, and stir altogether. The soup made precisely as above will be perfectly smooth and nice. Have little rolls or milk biscuits to eat with it.

This is a tomato soup of course best for impressing guests, whether for business or personal occasions.

Green Pea Soup

Make a nice soup, in the usual way, of beef, mutton, or knuckle of veal, cutting off all the fat, and using only the lean and the bones, allowing a quart of water to each pound of meat. If the meat is veal, add four or six calf's feet, which will greatly improve the soup. Boil it slowly, (having slightly seasoned it with pepper and salt,) and when it has boiled, and been well skimmed, and no more scum appears, then put in a quart or more of freshly-shelled green peas, with none among them that are old, hard, and yellow; and also a sprig or two of green mint, and a little loaf sugar.

Boil the peas till they are entirely dissolved. Then (having removed all the meat and bones) strain the soup through a sieve, and return it to the soup-pot, (which, in the meantime, should have been washed clean,) and stir into it a tea-cupful of green spinach juice, (obtained by pounding some spinach.) Have ready (boiled, or rather stewed in another pot) a quart of young fresh peas, enriched with a piece of fresh butter. These last peas should be boiled tender, but not to a mash. After they are in, give the soup another boil up, and then pour it off into a tureen, in the bottom of which has been laid some toast cut into square bits, with the crust removed. This soup should be of a fine green color, and very thick.

White Bean Soup

Early in the evening of the day before you make the soup, wash clean a large quart of dried white beans in a pan of cold water, and about bedtime pour off that water, and replace it with a fresh panful. Next morning, put on the beans to boil, with only water enough to cook them well, and keep them boiling slowly till they have all bursted, stirring them up frequently from the bottom, lest they should burn. Meantime, prepare in a larger pot, a good soup made of a shin of beef cut into pieces, and the hock of a cold ham, allowing a large quart of water to each pound of meat.

Season it with pepper only, (no salt,) and put in with it a head of celery, split and cut small. Boil the soup (skimming it well) till the meat is all in rags; then take it out, leaving not a morsel in the pot, and put in the boiled beans. Let them boil in the soup till they are undistinguishable, and the soup very thick. Put some small squares of toast in the bottom of a tureen, and pour the soup upon it.

There is said to be nothing better for making soup than the camp-kettle of the army. Many of the common soldiers make their bean soup of surpassing excellence.

Split pea soup - Image: Jeffreyw

Split Pea Soup

In buying dried or split peas, see that they are not old or worm eaten. Wash two quarts of them over night in two or three waters. In the morning make a rich soup of the lean of beef or mutton, and the hock of a ham. Season it with pepper, but no salt. When it has boiled, and been thoroughly skimmed, put in the split peas, with a head of celery cut into small pieces, or else two table-spoonfuls of celery seed.

Let it boil till the peas are entirely dissolved and undistinguishable. When it is finished strain the soup through a sieve, divesting it of the thin shreds of meat and bits of bone. Then transfer it to a tureen, in which has been laid some square bits of toast. Stir it up to the bottom directly before it goes to table.

You may boil in the soup (instead of the ham) a good piece (a rib piece, or a fillet) of corned pork, more lean than fat. When it is done, take the pork out of the soup, put it on a dish, and have ready to eat with it a pease pudding boiled by itself, cut in thick slices and laid round the pork. This pudding is made of a quart of split peas, soaked all night, mixed with four beaten eggs and a piece of fresh butter, and tied in a cloth and boiled three or four hours, or till the peas have become a mass.

Asparagus Soup

Make in the usual way a nice rich soup of beef or mutton, seasoned with salt and pepper. After it has been well boiled and skimmed, and the meat is all to pieces, strain the soup into another pot, or wash out the same, and return to it the liquid. Have ready a large quantity of fine fresh asparagus, with the stalks cut off close to the green tops or blossoms. It should have been lying in cold water all the time the meat was boiling.

Put into the soup half of the asparagus tops, and boil them in it till entirely dissolved, adding a tea-cupful of spinach juice, obtained by pounding fresh spinach in a mortar. Stir the juice well in and it will give a fine green color. Then add the remaining half of the asparagus; having previously boiled them in a small pan by themselves, till they are quite tender, but not till they lose their shape. Give the whole one boil up together. Make some nice slices of toast, (having cut off the crust.) Dip them for a minute in hot water. Butter them, lay them in the bottom of the tureen, and pour the soup upon them. This (like green peas) will do for company soup.

Cabbage Soup - Image: Mariuszjbie

Cabbage Soup

Remove the fat and bone from a good piece of fresh beef, or mutton—season it with a little salt and pepper, put it into a soup-pot, with a quart of water allowed to each pound of meat. Boil, and skim it till no more scum is seen on the surface. Then strain it, and thicken it with flour and butter mixed.

Have ready a fine fresh cabbage, (a young summer one is best) and after it is well washed through two cold waters, and all the leaves examined to see if any insects have crept between, quarter the cabbage, (removing the stalk) and with a cabbage-cutter, or a strong sharp knife, cut it into shreds. Or you may begin the cabbage whole and cut it into shreds, spirally, going round and round it with the knife. Put the cabbage into the clear soup, and boil it till, upon trial, by taking up a little on a fork, you find it quite tender and perfectly well cooked. Then serve it up in the tureen. This is a family soup.

Red Cabbage Soup

Red cabbages for soup should either be quartered, or cut into shreds; it is made in the same manner as cabbage soup, of beef or mutton, and seasoned with salt, pepper, and a jill of strong tarragon vinegar, or a table-spoonful of mixed tarragon leaves, if in summer. If the Russian variation of Borsch is desired, an accompaniment of diced beef should be added.

Fine Cabbage Soup

This fancier version of the cabbage stew is quite luxuriant, at the usual cost of time and complexity.

Remove the outside leaves from a fine, fresh, large cabbage. Cut the stalk short, and split it half-way down so as to divide the cabbage into quarters, but do not separate it quite to the bottom. Wash the cabbage, and lay it in cold water for half an hour or more. Then set it over the fire in a pot full of water, adding a little salt, and let it boil slowly for an hour and a half, or more—skimming it well. Then take it out, drain it, and laying it in a deep pan, pour on cold water, and let it remain till the cabbage is cold all through.

Next, having drained it from the cold water, cut the cabbage in shreds, (as for cold-slaw,) and put it into a clean pot containing a quart and a pint of boiling milk into which you have stirred a quarter of a pound of nice fresh butter, divided into four bits and rolled in flour, adding a little pepper and a very little salt. Boil it in the milk till thoroughly done and quite tender. Then make some nice toast, cut it into squares, lay it in the bottom of a tureen, and pour the soup on it. This being made without meat is a good soup for Lent. It will be improved by stirring in, towards the last, two or three beaten eggs.

Cauliflower Soup

Put into a soup-pot a knuckle of veal, and allow to each pound a quart of water. Add a set of calf's feet that have been singed and scraped, but not skinned; and the hock of a cold boiled ham. Boil it till all the meat is in rags, and the soup very thick, seasoning with cayenne and a few blades of mace, and adding, towards the last, some bits of fresh butter rolled in flour. Boil in another pot, one or two fine cauliflowers.

They are best boiled in milk. When quite done and very tender, drain them, cut off the largest stalks, and divide the blossoms into small pieces; put them into a deep covered dish, lay some fresh butter among them, and keep them hot till the veal soup is boiled to its utmost thickness. Then strain it into a soup-tureen, and put into it the cauliflower, grating some nutmeg upon it. This soup will be found very fine, and is an excellent white soup for company.

For Lent this soup may be made without meat, substituting milk, butter, and flour, and eggs, as in the receipt for fine cabbage soup. Season it with mace and nutmeg. If made with milk, &c., put no water on it, but boil the cauliflower in milk from the beginning. This can easily be done where milk is plenty.

Fine Onion Soup

Take a fine fresh neck of mutton, and to make a large tureen of soup, you must have a breast of mutton also. Let the meat be divided into chops, season it with a little salt, and put it in a soup-pot— allow a quart of water to each pound of mutton. Boil, and skim it till no more scum arises, and the meat drops in rags from the bones.

In a small pot boil in milk a dozen large onions, (or more,) adding pepper, mace, nutmeg, and some bits of fresh butter rolled in flour. The onions should previously be peeled and sliced. When they are quite soft, transfer them to the soup, with the milk, &c., in which they were cooked. Give them one boil in the soup. Then pour it off, or strain it into the tureen, omitting all the sediment, and bones, and shreds of meat. Make some nice slices of toast, dipping each in boiling water, and trimming off all the crust. Cut the toast into small squares, lay them in the bottom of the tureen, and pour the soup upon them. Where there is no objection to onions it will be much liked.

If milk is plenty use it instead of water for onion soup. White soups are always best when made with milk.

Turnip Stew

For a very small family take a neck of mutton, and divide it into steaks, omitting all the fat. For a family of moderate size, take a breast as well as a neck. Put them into a soup-pot with sufficient water to cover them, and let them stew till well browned. Skim them carefully.

Then pour on more water, in the proportion of a pint to each pound of meat, and add eight or ten turnips pared and sliced thin, with a very little pepper and salt. Let the soup boil till the turnips are all dissolved, and the meat in rags. Add, towards the last, some bits of butter rolled in flour, and in five minutes afterwards the soup will be done. Carefully remove all the bits of meat and bone before you send the soup to table. It will be found very good, and highly flavored with the turnips.

Onion soup may be made in the same manner. Parsnip soup also, cutting the parsnips into small bits. Or all three—turnips, onions and parsnips, may be used together.

Parsnip Soup

The meat for this soup may either be fresh beef, mutton, or fresh venison. Remove the fat, cut the meat into pieces, add a little salt, and put it into a soup-pot, with an allowance of rather less than a quart of water to each pound. Prepare some fine large parsnips, by first scraping and splitting them, and cutting them into pieces; then putting them into a frying pan, and frying them brown, in fresh butter or nice drippings.

When the soup has been boiled till the meat is all in rags, and well skimmed—put into it the fried parsnips and let them boil about ten minutes, but not till they break or go to pieces. Just before you put in the parsnips, stir in a table-spoonful of thickening made with butter and flour, mixed to a smooth paste. When you put it into the tureen to go to table, be sure to leave in the pot all the shreds of meat and bits of bone.

Carrot Soup

Take a good piece of fresh beef that has not been previously cooked. Remove the fat. It is of no use in making soup; and as it must all be skimmed off when boiling, it is better to clear it away before the meat goes into the pot. Season the beef with a very little salt and pepper, and allow a small quart of water to each pound.

Grate half a dozen or more large carrots on a coarse grater, and put them to boil in the soup with some other carrots; cut them into pieces about two inches long. When all the meat is boiled to rags, and has left the bone, pour off the soup from the sediment, transferring it to a tureen, and sending it to table with bread cut into it.

Potato Soup

Pare and slice thin half a dozen fine potatoes and a small onion. Boil them in three large pints of water, till so soft that you can pulp them through a colander. When returned to the pot add a very little salt and cayenne, and a quarter of a pound of fresh butter, divided into bits, and boil it ten minutes longer. When you put it into the tureen, stir in two table-spoonfuls or more of good cream. This is a soup for fast-days, or for invalids.

Beef and chestnut stew - Image: Krista

Chestnut Stew

Make, in the best manner, a stew of the lean of fresh beef, mutton, or venison, (seasoned with cayenne and a little salt,) allowing rather less than a quart of water to each pound of meat, skimming and boiling it well, till the meat is all in rags, and drops from the bone. Strain it, and put it into a clean pot. Have ready a quart or more of large chestnuts, boiled and peeled. If roasted, they will be still better. They should be the large Spanish chestnuts. Put the chestnuts into the soup, with some small bits of fresh butter rolled in flour. Boil the soup ten minutes longer, before it goes to table.

Portable Soup

This is a very good and nutritious soup, made first into a jelly, and then congealed into hard and viscous cakes, resembling glue. If well made, it will keep for many months in a cool, dry place, and when dissolved in hot water or gravy, will offer a fine liquid soup, very convenient to carry in a box on a journey or lengthy sea voyage, or to use in a remote place, where fresh meat for soup is not to be had. A piece of this glue, the size of a large walnut, will, when melted in water, become a pint bowl of soup; or by using less water, you may have it much richer. If there is time and opportunity, boil with the piece of soup a seasoning of sliced onion, sweet marjoram, sweet basil, or any herbs you choose. Also, a bit of butter rolled in flour.

To make portable soup, take two shins or legs of beef, two knuckles of veal, and four unskinned calves' feet. Have the bones broken or cracked. Put the whole into a large clean pot that will hold four gallons of water. Pour in, at beginning, only as much water as will cover the meat well, and set it over the fire, to heat gradually till it almost boils. Watch and skim it carefully while any scum rises. Then pour in a quart of cold water to make it throw up all the remaining scum, and then let it come to a good boil, continuing to skim as long as the least scum appears. In this be particular. When the liquid appears perfectly clear and free from grease, pour in the remainder of the water, and let it boil very gently for eight hours.

Strain it through a very clean hair sieve into a large stoneware pan, and set it where it will cool quickly. Next day, remove all the remaining grease, and pour the liquid, as quickly as possible, into a three-gallon stew-pan, taking care not to disturb the settlings at the bottom. Keep the pan uncovered, and let it boil as fast as possible over a quick fire. Next, transfer it to a three-quart stew-pan, and skim it again, if necessary. Watch it well, and see that it does not burn, as that would spoil the whole. Take out a little in a spoon, and hold it in the air, to see if it will jelly. If it will not, boil it a little longer. Till it jellies, it is not done.

Have ready some small white ware preserve pots, clean, and quite dry. Fill them with the soup, and let them stand undisturbed till next day. Set, over a slow fire, a large flat-bottomed stew-pan, one-third filled with boiling water. Place in it the pots of soup, seeing it does not reach within two inches of their rims. Let the pots stand uncovered in this water, hot, but without boiling, for six or seven hours. This will bring the soup to a proper thickness, which should be that of a stiff jelly, when hot; and when cold, it should be like hard glue. When finished turn out the moulds of soup, and wrap them up separately in new brownish paper, and put them up in boxes, breaking off a piece when wanted to dissolve the soup.

Portable soup may be improved by the addition of three pounds of nice lean beef, to the shins, knuckles, calves' feet. The beef must be cut into bits.

If you have any friends going the overland journey to the Pacific, a box of portable soup may be a most useful present to them.

Pepper Pot Stew

Have ready a small half pound of very nice white tripe, that has been thoroughly boiled and skinned, in a pot by itself, till quite soft and tender. It should be cut into very small strips or mouthfuls. Put into another pot a neck of mutton, and a pound of lean ham, and pour on it a large gallon of water. Boil it slowly, and skim it.

When the scum has ceased to rise, put in two large onions sliced, four potatos quartered, and four sliced turnips. Season with a very small piece of red pepper or capsicum, taking care not to make it too hot. Then add the boiled tripe. Make a quart bowlful of small dumplings of butter and flour, mixed with a very little water; and throw them into the pepper-pot, which should afterwards boil about an hour. Then take it up, and remove the meat before it is put into the tureen. Leave in the bits of tripe.

Noodle Soup

This soup may be made with either beef or mutton, but the meat must be fresh for the purpose, and not cold meat, re-cooked. Cut off all the fat, and break the bones. If boiled in the soup they improve it. To each pound of meat allow a small quart of water.

Boil and skim it, till the meat drops from the bone. Put in with the meat, after the scum has ceased to rise, some turnips, carrots and onions, cut in slices, and boil them till all to pieces.

Strain the soup, and return the liquid to a clean pot. Have ready a large quantity of noodles and put them into the strained soup; let them boil in it ten minutes. The noodles are composed of beaten eggs, made into a paste or dough, with flour and a very little fresh butter. This paste is rolled out thin into a square sheet. This sheet is then closely rolled up like a scroll or quire of thick paper, and then with a sharp knife cut round into shreds, or shavings, as cabbage is cut for slaw. These cuttings must be dredged with flour to prevent their sticking. Throw them into the soup while boiling the second time, and let it boil for ten minutes longer.

Duck Soup

Half roast a pair of fine large tame ducks, keeping them half an hour at the fire, and saving the gravy, the fat of which must be carefully skimmed off. Then cut them up; season them with black pepper; and put them into a soup-pot with four or five small onions sliced thin, a small bunch of sage, a thin slice of cold ham cut into pieces, a grated nutmeg, and the yellow rind of a lemon grated. Add the gravy of the ducks. Pour on, slowly, three quarts of boiling water from a kettle. Cover the soup-pot, and set it over a moderate fire. Simmer it slowly (skimming it well) for about four hours, or till the flesh of the ducks is dissolved into small shreds. When done, strain it through a tureen, the bottom of which is covered with toasted bread, cut into square dice about two inches in size.

French White Soup

Boil a knuckle of veal and four calves' feet in five quarts of water, with three onions sliced, a bunch of sweet herbs, four heads of white celery cut small, a table-spoonful of whole pepper, and a small tea-spoonful of salt, adding five or six large blades of mace.

Let it boil very slowly, till the meat is in rags and has dropped from the bone, and till the gristle has quite dissolved. Skim it well while boiling. When done, strain it through a sieve into a tureen, or a deep white-ware pan.

Next day, take off all the fat, and put the jelly (for such it ought to be) into a clean soup-pot with two ounces of vermicelli, and set it over the fire. When the vermicelli is dissolved, stir in, gradually, a pint of thick cream, while the soup is quite hot; but do not let it come to a boil after the cream is in, lest it should curdle. Cut up one or two French rolls in the bottom of a tureen, pour in the soup, and send it to table.

Cocoa-Nut Soup

Take eight calves' feet (two sets) that have been scalded and scraped, but not skinned; and put them into a soup-kettle with six or seven blades of mace, and the yellow rind of a lemon grated. Pour on a gallon of water; cover the kettle, and let it boil very slowly (skimming it well) till the flesh is reduced to rags and has dropped entirely from the bones. Then strain it into a broad white-ware pan, and set it away to get cold.

When it has congealed, scrape off the fat and sediment, cut up the cake of jelly, (or stock,) and put it into a clean porcelain or enamelled kettle. Have ready half a pound of very finely grated cocoa-nut. Mix it with a pint of cream. If you cannot obtain cream, take rich unskimmed milk, and add to it three ounces of the best fresh butter divided into three parts, each bit rolled in arrow-root or rice-flour.

Mix it, gradually, with the cocoa-nut, and add it to the calves-feet-stock in the kettle, seasoned with a small nutmeg grated. Set it over the fire, and boil it, slowly, about a quarter of an hour; stirring it well. Then transfer it to a tureen, and serve it up. Have ready small French rolls, or light milk biscuit to eat with it; also powdered sugar in case any of the company should wish to sweeten it.

Almond Soup

This is made in the above manner, substituting pounded almonds for the grated cocoa-nut. You must have half a pound of shelled sweet almonds, mixed with two ounces of shelled bitter almonds. After blanching them in hot water, they must be pounded to a smooth paste (one at a time) in a marble mortar; adding frequently a little rose-water to prevent their oiling, and becoming heavy. Or you may use peach-water for this purpose; in which case omit the bitter almonds, as the peach-water will give the desired flavor. When the pounded almonds are ready, mix them with the other ingredients, as above.

The calves' feet for these soups should be boiled either very early in the morning, or the day before.

The four seasons - Image: Masakazu Matsumoto

Seasonal Soups

The following four soups are ideal for each of the seasons, being made from ingredients widely available and corresponding well to each season. Just as the spring and summer soups are refreshing and light, ideal for consuming from a flask in the park or on a bright day's jog, so is the winter stew wholesome and warming for the inclement times.

Springtime Soup

Unless your dinner hour is very late, the stock for this soup should be made the day before it is wanted, and set away in a stone pan, closely covered. To make the stock take a knuckle of veal, break the bones, and cut it into several pieces. Allow a quart of water to each pound of veal.

Put it into a soup-pot, with a set of calves' feet and some bits of cold ham, cut off near the hock. If you have no ham, sprinkle in a tea-spoonful of salt, and a salt-spoon of cayenne. Place the pot over a moderate fire, and let it simmer slowly (skimming it well) for several hours, till the veal is all to rags and the flesh of the calves' feet has dropped in shreds from the bones. Then strain the soup; and if not wanted that day, set it away in a stone pan, as above mentioned.

Next day have, ready boiled, two quarts or more of green peas, (they must on no account be old,) and a pint of the green tops cut off from asparagus boiled for the purpose. Pound a handful of raw spinach till you have extracted a tea-cupful of the juice. Set the soup or stock over the fire; add the peas, asparagus, and spinach juice, stirring them well in; also a quarter of a pound of fresh butter, divided into four bits, and rolled in flour. Let the whole come to a boil; and then take it off and transfer it to a tureen. It will be found excellent.

In boiling the peas for this soup, you may put with them half a dozen sprigs of green mint, to be afterwards taken out.

Late in the spring you may add to the other vegetables two cucumbers, pared and sliced, and the whitest part or heart of a lettuce, boiled together; then well drained, and put into the soup with the peas and asparagus. It must be very thick with vegetables.

Summertime Soup

Take a large neck of mutton, and hack it so as nearly to cut it apart, but not quite. Allow a small quart of water to each pound of meat, and sprinkle on a tea-spoonful of salt and a very little black pepper. Put it into a soup-pot, and boil it slowly (skimming it well) till the meat is reduced to rags. Then strain the liquid, return it to the soup-pot, and carefully remove all the fat from the surface.

Have ready half a dozen small turnips sliced thin, two young onions sliced, a table-spoonful of sweet marjoram leaves picked from the stalks, and a quart of shelled Lima beans. Put in the vegetables, and boil them in the soup till they are thoroughly done. You may add to them two table-spoonfuls of green nasturtium seeds, either fresh or pickled. Put in also some little dumplings, (made of flour and butter,) about ten minutes before the soup is done.

Instead of Lima beans, you may divide a cauliflower or two broccolis into sprigs, and boil them in the soup with the other vegetables.

This soup may be made of a shoulder of mutton, cut into pieces and the bones cracked. For a large potful add also the breast to the neck, cutting the bones apart.

Autumn Soup

Begin this soup as early in the day as possible. Take six pounds of the lean of fine fresh beef; cut it into small pieces; sprinkle it with a tea-spoonful of salt, (not more); put it into a soup-pot, and pour on six quarts of water. The hock of a cold ham will greatly improve it. Set it over a moderate fire, and let it boil slowly.

After it comes to a boil, skim it well. Have ready a quarter of a peck of okras cut into very thin round slices, and a quarter of a kilo of tomatoes cut into pieces; also a quart of shelled Lima beans. Season them with pepper. Put them in; and after the whole has boiled three hours at least, take four ears of young Indian corn, and having grated off all the grains, add them to the soup and boil it an hour longer. Before you serve up the soup remove from it all the bits of meat, which, if the soup is sufficiently cooked, will be reduced to shreds. You may put in with the okras and tomatoes one or two sliced onions. The soup, when done, should be as thick as a jelly.

Okras for soup may be kept all winter, by tying them separately to a line stretched high across the store room.

Wintertime Soup

The day before you make the soup, get a leg or shin of beef. Have the bone sawed through in several places, and the meat notched or scored down to the bone. This will cause the juice or essence to come out more freely, when cooked. Rub it slightly with salt; cover it, and set it away. Next morning, early as possible, as soon as the fire is well made up, put the beef into a large soup-pot, allowing to each pound a small quart of water.

Then taste the water, and if the salt that has been rubbed on the meat is not sufficient, add a very little more. Throw in also a tea-spoonful of whole pepper-corns; and you may add half a dozen blades of mace. Let it simmer slowly till it comes to a boil; then skim it well. After it boils, you may quicken the fire. At nine o'clock put in a large head of cabbage cut fine as for cold-slaw; six carrots grated; the leaves stripped from a bunch of sweet marjoram; and the leaves of a sprig of parsley.

An hour afterwards, add six turnips, and three potatoes, all cut into four or eight pieces. Also two onions, which will be better if previously roasted brown, and then sliced. Continue to keep the soup on a steady, but not hard, simmer unless the dinner hour is very early. For a late dinner, there will be time to boil it slowly all the while; and all soups are the better for long and slow boiling. See that it is well skimmed, so that, when done, there will be not a particle of fat or scum on the surface. At dinner-time take it up with a large ladle, and transfer it to a tureen.

In doing so, carefully avoid the shreds of meat and bone. Leave them all in the bottom of the pot, pressing them down with the ladle. A mass of shreds in the tureen or soup-plate looks slovenly and disgusting, and should never be seen at the table; also, they absorb too much of the liquid. Let the vegetables remain in the soup when it is served up, but pick out every shred of meat or bone that may be found in the tureen when ready to go to table.

In very cold weather, what is left of this soup will keep till the second day; when it must be simmered again over the fire, till it just comes to a boil. Put it away in a tin or stone vessel. The lead which is used in glazing earthen jars frequently communicates its poison to liquids that are kept in them.

Rich Vegetable Soup

This quality soup confers the richest tastes Soak all night, in cold water, either two quarts of yellow split peas, or two quarts of dried white beans. In the morning drain them, and season them with a very little salt and cayenne, and a head of minced celery, or else a heaped table-spoonful of celery seed. Put them into a soup-pot with four quarts of water, and boil them slowly till they are all dissolved and undistinguishable. Stir them frequently.

Have ready a profuse quantity of fresh vegetables, such as turnips, carrots, parsnips, potatos, onions, and cauliflowers; also, salsify, and asparagus tops. Put in, first, the vegetables that require the longest boiling. They should all be cut into small pieces. Enrich the whole with some bits of fresh butter rolled in flour. Boil these vegetables in the soup till they are all quite tender. Then transfer it to a tureen, and serve it up hot.

The foundation being of dried peas or beans, makes it very thick and smooth, and the fresh vegetables improve its flavor. It is a good soup for Lent, or for any time, if properly and liberally made.

All vegetable soups can be made in Lent without meat, if milk is substituted for water, and with butter, beaten eggs and spice, to flavor and enrich it.

French Pot Au Feu

This is one of the national dishes of France. The following is a genuine French receipt, and it would be found very palatable and very convenient if tried in our own land of plenty. The true French way to cook it is in an earthen pipkin, such as can be had in any pottery shop.

The French vessel has a wide mouth, and close-fitting lid, with a handle at each side, in the form of circular ears. It is large and swelling in the middle, and narrows down towards the bottom. The American pipkin has a short thick spout at one side, and stands on three or four low feet. No kitchen should be without these vessels, which are cheap, very strong, and easily kept clean. They can sit on a stove, or in the corner of the fire, and are excellent for slow cooking.

The wife of a French artisan commences her pot au feu soon after breakfast, prepares the ingredients, puts them, by degrees, into the pot, attends to it during the day; and when her husband has done his work she has ready for him an excellent and substantial repast, far superior to what in our country is called a tea-dinner. Men frequently indemnify themselves for the poorness of a tea-dinner by taking a dram of whiskey afterwards. A Frenchman is satisfied with his excellent pot au feu and some fruit afterwards. The French are noted as a temperate nation. If they have eaten to their satisfaction they have little craving for drink. Yet there is no country in the world where so much good eating might be had as in America, and it is there where the Pot au Feu has come into its wholesome own.

Making in quantity

For a large pot au feu, put into the pan six pounds of good fresh beef cut up, and pour on it four quarts of water. Set it near the fire, skim it when it simmers, and when nearly boiling, add a tea-spoonful of salt, half a pound of liver cut in pieces, and some black pepper. Then add two or three large carrots, sliced or grated on a coarse grater; four turnips, pared and quartered; eight young onions peeled and sliced thick, two of the onions roasted whole; a head of celery cut up; a parsnip split and cut up; and six potatoes, pared, sliced, or quartered.

In short any good vegetables now in season, including tomatoes in summer and autumn. Also a bunch of sweet herbs, chopped small. Let the whole continue to boil slowly and steadily; remembering to skim well. Let it simmer slowly five or six hours. Then, having laid some large slices of bread in the bottom of a tureen, or a very large pan or bowl, pour the stew or soup upon it; all the meat, and all the vegetables. If you have any left, recook it the next morning for breakfast, and that day you may prepare something else for dinner.

For beef you may substitute mutton, or fresh venison, if you live in a venison country, and can get it newly slaughtered.

Wild Duck Soup

This is a company soup. If you live where wild ducks are abundant, it will afford an agreeable variety occasionally to make soup of some of them. If you suspect them to be sedgy or fishy, (you can ascertain by the smell when drawing or cleaning them,) parboil each duck, with a carrot put into his body. Then take out the carrot and throw it away. You will find that the unpleasant flavor has left the ducks, and been entirely absorbed by the carrots. To make the soup—cut up the ducks, season the pieces with a little salt and pepper, and lay them in a soup-pot.

For a good pot of soup you should have four wild ducks. Add two or three sliced onions, and a table-spoonful of minced sage. Also a quarter of a pound of butter divided into four, and each piece rolled in flour. Pour in water enough to make a rich soup, and let it boil slowly till all the flesh has left the bones,— skim it well. Thicken it with boiled or roasted chestnuts, peeled, and then mashed with a potato beetle. A glass of Madeira or sherry will be found an improvement, stirred in at the last, or the juice and grated peel of a lemon. In taking it up for the tureen, be careful to leave all the bones and bits of meat in the bottom of the pot.

Venison stew, sans dumplings - Image: Jason Reidy

Venison Stew

Take a large fine piece of fresh venison. It is best at the season when the deer are fat and juicy, from having plenty of wild berries to feed on. I do not consider winter-venison worth eating, when the meat is poor and hard, and affords no gravy, and also is black from being kept too long.

When venison is fresh and in good order it yields a fine soup, allowing a small quart of water to each pound of meat. When it has boiled well, and been skimmed, put in some small dumplings made of flour and minced suet, or drippings. Also, boiled sweet potatoes, cut into round thick slices. You may add boiled sweet corn cut off the cob; and, indeed, whatever vegetables are in season. The soup-meat should boil till all the flesh is loose on the bones, and the bits and shreds should not be served up.

Game Soup

Take partridges, pheasants, grouse, quails, or any of the birds considered as game. You may put in here as many different sorts as you can procure. They must all be fresh. When they are cleaned and plucked, cut them in pieces as for carving, and put them into a soup-pot, with four calves' feet and some slices of ham, two sticks of celery, and a bundle of sweet herbs chopped small, and water enough to cover the whole well. Boil and skim well, till all the flesh is loose from the bones. Strain the liquid through a sieve into a clean pot, then thicken it with fresh butter rolled in flour. Add some force-meat balls that have been already fried; or else some hard-boiled yolks of eggs; some currant jelly, or some good wine into which a half-nutmeg has been grated; the juice of two oranges or lemons, and the grated yellow peel of one lemon. Give the soup another boil up, and then send it to table, having bread rolls to eat with it.

This is a fine soup for company. Venison soup may be made in this manner. Hare soup also.

Squatter's Soup

Take plenty of freshly slaughtered venison, as fat and juicy as you can get it. Cut the meat off the bones and put it (with the bones) into a large pot. Season it with pepper and salt, and pour on sufficient water to make a good rich soup. Boil it slowly (remembering to skim it well) till the meat is all in rags. Have ready some ears of young sweet corn. Boil them in a pot by themselves till they are quite soft. Cut the grains off the cob into a deep dish.

Having cleared the soup from shreds and bits of bone left at the bottom of the pot, stir in a thickening made of Indian meal mixed to a paste with a little fresh lard, or venison gravy. And afterwards throw in, by degrees, the cut corn. Let all boil together, till the corn is soft, or for about half an hour. Then take it up in a large pan. It will be found very good by persons who never were squatters. This soup, with a wild turkey or a buffalo hump roasted, and stewed grapes sweetened well with maple sugar, will make a good backwoods dinner.

Mock turtle soup - Image: Wilfried Wittkowsky

Mock Turtle Soup

Boil together a knuckle of veal (cut up) and a set of calves' feet, split. Also the hock of a cold boiled ham. Season it with cayenne pepper; but the ham will render it salt enough. You may add a smoked tongue. Allow, to each pound of meat, a small quart of water. After the meat has come to a boil and been well skimmed, add half a dozen sliced parsnips, three sliced onions, and a head of celery cut small, with a large bunch of sweet marjoram, and two large carrots sliced. Boil all together till the vegetables are nearly dissolved and the meat falls from the bone.

Then strain the whole through a colander, and transfer the liquid to a clean pot. Have ready some fine large sweetbreads that have been soaked in warm water for an hour till all the blood was disgorged; then transferred to boiling water for ten minutes, and then taken out and laid in very cold water. This will blanch them, and all sweetbreads should look white. Take them out; and remove carefully all the pipe or gristle. Cut the sweetbreads in pieces or mouthfuls, and put them into the pot of strained soup. Have ready about two or three dozen (or more) of force-meat balls, made of cold minced veal and ham seasoned with nutmeg and mace, enriched with butter, and mixed with grated lemon-peel, bread-crumbs, chopped marjoram and beaten eggs, to make the whole into smooth balls about the size of a hickory nut. Throw the balls into the soup, and add a fresh lemon, sliced thin, and a pint of Madeira wine. Give it one more boil up; then put it into a tureen and send it to table.

This ought to be a rich soup, and is seldom made except for dinner company.

If the above method is exactly followed, there will be found no necessity for taking the trouble and enduring the disgust and tediousness of cleaning and preparing a calf's head for mock turtle soup—a very unpleasant process, which too much resembles the horrors of a dissecting room. And when all is done a calf's head is a very insipid article.

It will be found that the above is superior to any mock turtle. Made of shin beef, with all these ingredients, it is very rich and fine.

Paila marina - a popular fish stew variant from Chile - Image: Daniel Norero Fecha

Fish Soup

All fish soups should be made with milk, (if unskimmed so much the better,) using no water whatever. The best fish for soup are the small sort of cat-fish; also tutaug, porgie, blue fish, white fish, black fish or sea-bass. Cut off their heads, tails, and fins, and remove the skin, and the backbone, and cut the fish into pieces. To each pound of fish allow a quart of rich milk.

Put into the soup-pot some pieces of cold boiled ham. No salt will then be required; but season with cayenne pepper, and a few blades of mace and some grated nutmeg. Add a bunch of sweet marjoram, the leaves stripped from the stalks and chopped. Make some little dumplings of flour and butter, and put them in when the soup is about half done. Half an hour's steady boiling will be sufficient. Serve up in the tureen the pieces of fish and ham. Also some toast cut in dice.

Soup may be made in this manner, of chickens or rabbits, using always milk enriched with bits of butter rolled in flour and flavored with bits of cold ham.

Lobster Soup

This is a fine soup for company. Take two or three fine fresh lobsters, (the middle sized are the best.) Heat a large pot of water, throwing in a large handful of salt. When it is boiling hard put in the lobsters, head foremost, that they may die immediately. They will require at least half an hour's fast boiling; if large, three quarters. When done, take them out, wipe off the scum that has collected on the shell, and drain the lobster. First break off the large claws, and crack them, then split the body, and extract all the white meat, and the red coral—nothing else—and cut it into small pieces. Mash the coral into smooth bits with the back of a large spoon, mixing with it plenty of sweet oil; and, gradually, adding it to the bits of chopped lobster.

Put into a clear soup-pot two quarts, or more, of good milk, and thicken it with half a dozen crackers or butter-biscuit, pounded fine; or the grated crumbs of two or three small rolls, and stir in a quarter of a pound of fresh butter made into a paste with two spoonfuls of flour. Put in the chopped lobster, seasoned with nutmeg, a few blades of mace powdered, and a little cayenne. Let all boil together, slowly, for half an hour, keeping it closely covered. Towards the last, stir in two beaten eggs. Lay some very small soda biscuit in the bottom of a tureen, and pour the soup upon them. Nasturtion flowers strewed at the last thickly over the surface of this soup, when in the tureen, are an improvement both to its appearance and flavor. So is peppergrass.

Crab Soup

Take the meat of two dozen boiled crabs, cut it small, and give it a boil in two quarts of milk. Season it with powdered mace, nutmeg, and a little cayenne, and thicken it with butter mixed in flour; or, make the flour and butter into little dumplings. Have ready half a dozen yolks of hard-boiled eggs, and crumble them into the soup just before you take it from the fire. Add the heart of a fresh green lettuce, cut small and strewed over the surface of the soup, after it is poured into the tureen.

Oyster Soup

Strain the liquor from one hundred oysters, and carefully remove any bits of shell or particles of sea-weed. To every pint of oyster liquor allow an equal quantity of rich milk. Season it with whole pepper and some blades of mace. Add a head of celery, washed, scraped, and minced small. Put the whole into a soup-pot, and boil and skim it well. When it boils put in the oysters.

Also, a quarter of a pound of fresh butter; divide into four pieces, each piece rolled in flour. If you can procure cream, add a half-pint, otherwise boil some six eggs hard, and crumble the yolks into the soup. After the oysters are in give them but one boil up, just sufficient to plump them. If boiled longer they will shrink and shrivel and lose their taste. Take them all out and set them away to cool. When the soup is done, place in the bottom of the tureen some small square pieces of nicely toasted bread cut into dice, and pour on the soup; grate in a nutmeg and then add the oysters. Serve it up very hot.

Another way is to chop or cut small the oysters, omitting the hard part. Make the soup as above, and put in the minced oysters at the last, letting them boil but five minutes. Mix the powdered nutmeg with them. This is a good way, if you make but a small quantity of soup.

Image: 木更津乃風

Clam Soup

Having washed clean the outside shells of a hundred small sand clams, (or scrubbed them with a brush,) put them into a large pot of boiling water. When they open their shells take them out with a ladle, and as you do so, put them into a colander to drain off the liquor. Then extract the clams from the shells with a knife. Save a quart of the liquor, putting the clams in a pitcher by themselves. Mix with the quart of liquor, in a clean pot, two quarts of rich milk. Put in the clams, and add some pepper-corns and some blades of mace.

113

Also, a bunch of sweet marjoram, the leaves stripped off and minced. After all has boiled well for an hour, add half a pound, or more, of nice fresh butter, made into little dumplings with flour; also a pint of grated bread-crumbs. Let it boil a quarter of an hour longer. Then pour the soup off from the clams and leave them in the bottom of the pot. They will not now be worth eating. If you cannot obtain small clams, you may cut large ones in pieces, but they are very coarse and tough.

Fast Daytime Soup

This is a wintertime soup ideal for warming up in.

Having soaked all night two quarts of split peas, put them into a soup-pot, adding a sliced onion, two heads of celery, the stalks split and cut small; a table-spoonful of chopped mint, another of marjoram, and two beets, that have been previously boiled and sliced. Mix all these with half a pound of fresh butter cut into pieces and dredged with flour. Season with a little salt and pepper. Pour on rather more than water enough to cover the whole. Let them boil till all the things are quite tender, and the peas dissolved. When done, cover the bottom of a tureen with small square bits of toast, and pour in the contents of the soup-pot.

It is a good way to boil the split peas in a pot by themselves, till they are quite dissolved, and then add them to the ingredients in the other pot.

Vegetable soups require a large portion of vegetables, and butter always, as a substitute for meat.

Friday Soup

This is a delicious soup, easily and quickly prepared and ideal for the warmer months.

Pare and slice six cucumbers, and cut up the white part or heart of six lettuces; slice two onions, and cut small the leaves of six sprigs of fresh green mint, unless mint is disliked by the persons that are to eat the soup; in which case, substitute parsley. Add a quart of young green peas. Put the whole into a soup-pot, with as much water as will more than cover them well. Season slightly with salt and a little cayenne, and add half a pound of nice fresh butter, divided into six, each piece dredged well with flour. Boil the whole for an hour and a half. Then serve it up, without straining; having colored it green with a tea-cup of pounded spinach juice.

When green peas are out of season, you may substitute tomatoes peeled and quartered.

This soup, having no meat, is chiefly for fast days, but will be found good at any time.

Baked Soup

On the days that you bake or buy freshly baked bread, you may have a dish of thick soup with very little trouble, by putting into a large earthen jug or covered pan, the following articles:

Two pounds of fresh beef, or mutton, cut into small slices, having first removed the fat; two sliced onions and four carrots, and four parsnips cut in four; also, four turnips, six potatoes pared and cut up, and half a dozen tomatoes, peeled and quartered. Season the whole with a little salt and pepper. A large beet, scraped and cut up, will be an improvement.

To these things pour on three quarts of water. Cover the earthen vessel, and set it in the oven with the bread, and let the soup bake at the same time.

If the bread is done before the dinner hour, you must keep the soup still longer in the oven.

Do not use cold meat for this or any other soup, unless you are very poor.

Conclusion

The examples within this book are but a fair introduction to the more popular soups found in the West. The Eastern pantheon of soups has been left nearly untouched, with inspiration drawn upon only sparsely. While we've done a little more than scratch the proverbial surface, there is plenty of variation and ideas out there to sustain any host, aspiring cook or casual culinary enthusiast for years.

It is my hope however that from the basic descriptions and templates for soups and stews writ within this small manual that you will be inspired to invent and create your own elaborations, or seek out others already created. I have a conviction that soups and stews are the most important of meals; together with their beneficent effects during illness, they always form the beginning of a dining experience – without a good start, they can be no good end; if the first taste isn't to your liking, it colors your opinion of a place forever.

Despite my personal devotion to tradition, there is much to be said for the modern styles of soup and stew, particularly those appearing in the classier of televised cookery shows or in restaurants which value the entrée well-made. The utility of the soup has been further helped by flasks which can keep a stew warm for a good day or so.

For now, your foundations are present, and I wish you the best of luck in soup and stew cookery.

CPSIA information can be obtained
at www.ICGtesting.com
Printed in the USA
FSHW010755091218
54346FS